Brexit?

Brexit?

Stefano Francesco Fugazzi

Faber est suae quisque fortunae

Copyright © 2015 Stefano Fugazzi

All rights reserved. This book or any portion thereof may not be reproduced or used in any manner whatsoever without the express written permission of the publisher except for the use of brief quotations in a book review or scholarly journal.

First edition: June 2015
ISBN 978-1-326-31174-2

Published by **ABC Economics**
Website: http://abceconomics.com/
Email: abc.economics@yahoo.com

Printed in the United Kingdom

Friendship may, and often does, grow into love, but love never subsides into friendship.

Lord Byron

Contents

Introduction	1
Section 1 – UK macroeconomic indicators	5
Section 2 – Reasons to stay in or leave the EU	17
Section 3 – The legal framework	25
Section 4 – The economic impact of Brexit	47
Bibliography	77

INTRODUCTION

Before the 2015 general election took place, the Conservatives pledged in their manifesto to legislate for a referendum on EU membership to be held by the end of 2017. Following the election of a Conservative majority government on May 7th, Cameron reiterated that same pledge, suggesting that the referendum could even take place a year before than originally planned. The government included the referendum proposal in the Queen's speech on May 27th.

***

Should Britain vote in favour of 'Brexit', it would not be the first country to leave Europe, since as far back as 1985 Greenland withdrew from the then European Community (EC) after obtaining a high degree of self-determination from Denmark in 1979.

Greenland residents held a referendum in February 1982 on whether to stay in the EC: 52% of the voters opted to discontinue their country's membership. At that time the Greenland Government and the Danish Government first, then the Danish Government and the European Commission, held difficult and protracted negotiations, particularly with regard to fisheries. Exit terms were eventually agreed by the Council of Europe on 20 February 1984, a decision which prompted Greenland's withdrawal from the EEC on 1 February 1985. Following the exit, Greenland became associated with the EU as an Overseas Country and Territory (OCT) in conformity with the Greenland Treaty.

The legal foundation for Greenland's withdrawal from the EC was the former Article 236 of the Treaty of Rome, which authorised amendments to the EC Treaty (*"the Government of any Member State or the Commission may submit to the Council proposals for the amendment of this Treaty"*) and entered into force following ratification by all Member States *"in accordance with their respective constitutional requirements"*.

Greenland was granted special status as the country continued to receive European funding after its withdrawal and had tariff-free access to the common market for fisheries products in exchange for EC access to Greenland waters.

***

Given Britain's role and influence in Europe, it would be safe to assume that both litigant parties, namely the UK and the EU, will try to 'save the marriage' before coming to the point of splitting up.

A best case scenario would see Cameron renegotiating changes to the EU treaties ahead of the referendum. If the Prime Minister's EU negotiations are to be judged as a success, the forthcoming referendum should not simply be a vote to approve or reject a list of concessions to the UK, but rather a mandate for a path to implement substantial reforms.

The target should be a new settlement that leads to a genuine change of direction of Britain's relationship with the EU. It may not be possible to achieve everything before the referendum is held but, in order to avoid the Yes or No party obtaining a narrow victory, which would only estrange half of the British electorate, fundamental reforms are needed, which manage to establish a path to a multi-form EU.

According to Open Europe, an independent think tank, in order to win the negotiations with the European Union on treaty change, the UK needs to target a series of 11 reforms under three fundamental headings – Flexibility and the rights of non-Eurozone states; Competitiveness; Democratic accountability.[1]

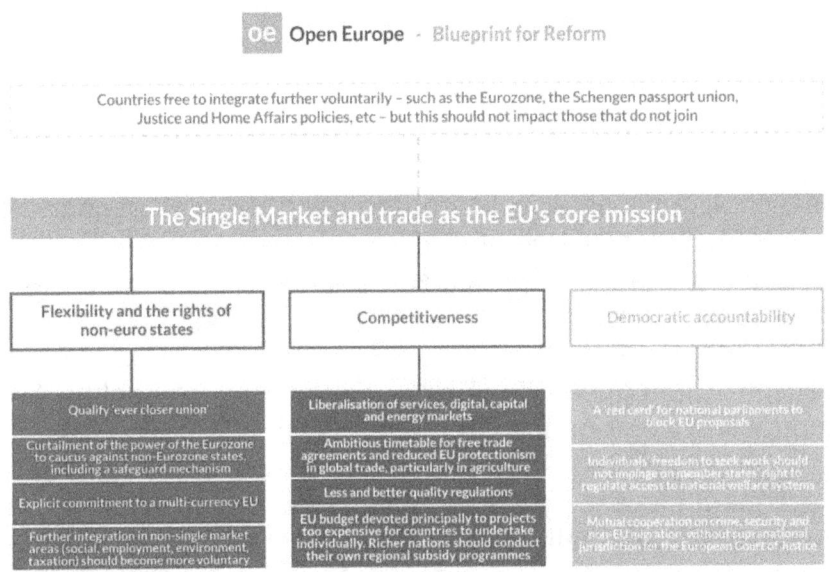

The reader should note that even in the event of Brexit, it is likely that some time will pass before the UK actually leaves the EU. This is due to the fact that Article 50 of the Treaty of Lisbon states that in this case both parties, the UK and the EU, would need up to two years in order to complete the negotiation process, which sets forth both the terms of the exit and the transitional arrangements that must be put in place before the union is effectively broken.

---

[1] Open Europe, "A blueprint for reform of the European Union", June 2015

Additionally, Article 50 of the Lisbon Treaty clearly states that the leaving country will need to consider *"the framework for [a State's] future relationship with the Union"*, which implies that departure from the EU does not necessarily mean that Britain will cease any relationship with the European Union but rather, it would simply change its status from EU to EEA (or EFTA) member.

***

The remainder of this paper is organised as follows.

Section 1 provides a review of the main UK macroeconomic indicators since the year 2000; a 5-year forecast for the 2015-2019 period and some statistics on the UK trade balance with the EU.

Section 2 introduces the Brexit dilemma by presenting two contrasting views on the UK membership.

Sections 3 focuses on the legal framework of the EU treaties and possible alternatives to EU membership.

Finally, Section 4 presents a number studies which assess the potential impact of Brexit on the UK economy.

Stefano Francesco Fugazzi
abceconomics.com

SECTION 1:
UK MACROECONOMIC INDICATORS

UK key economic indicators (2000-2014)

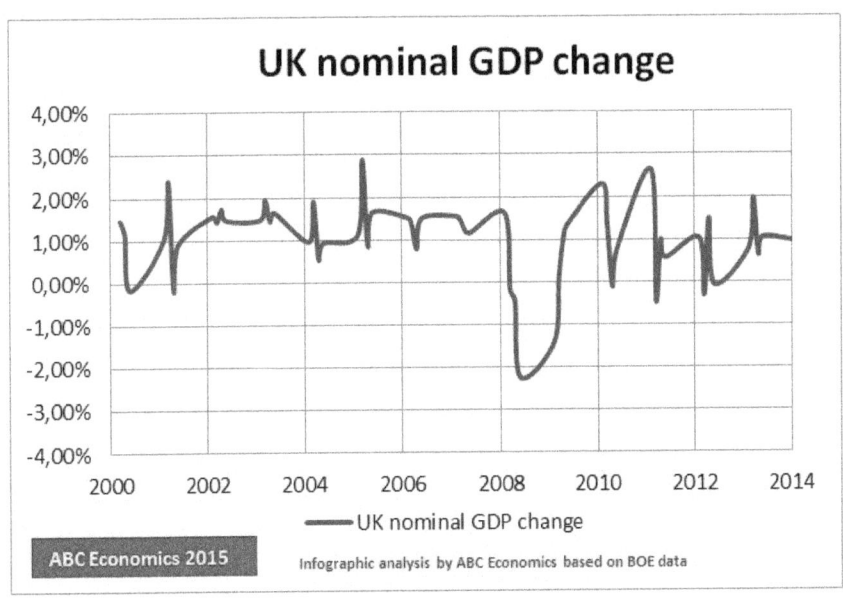

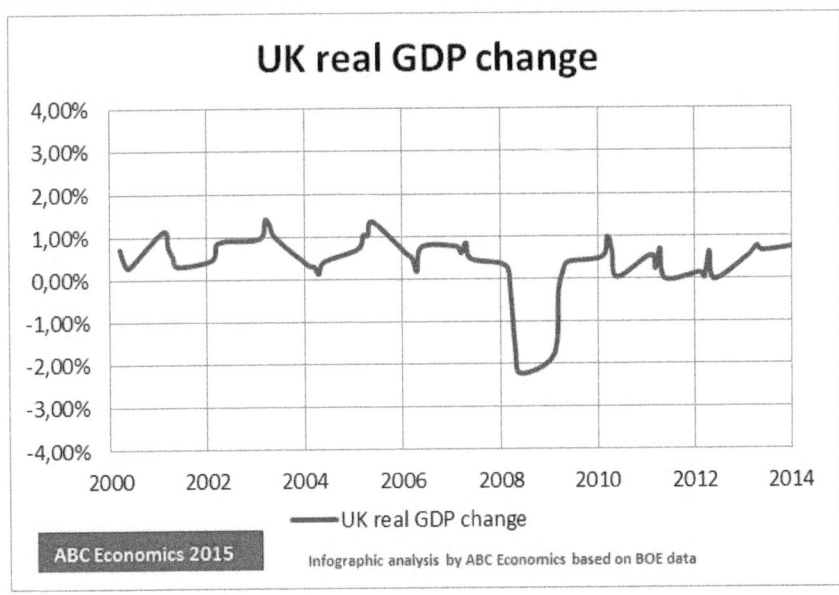

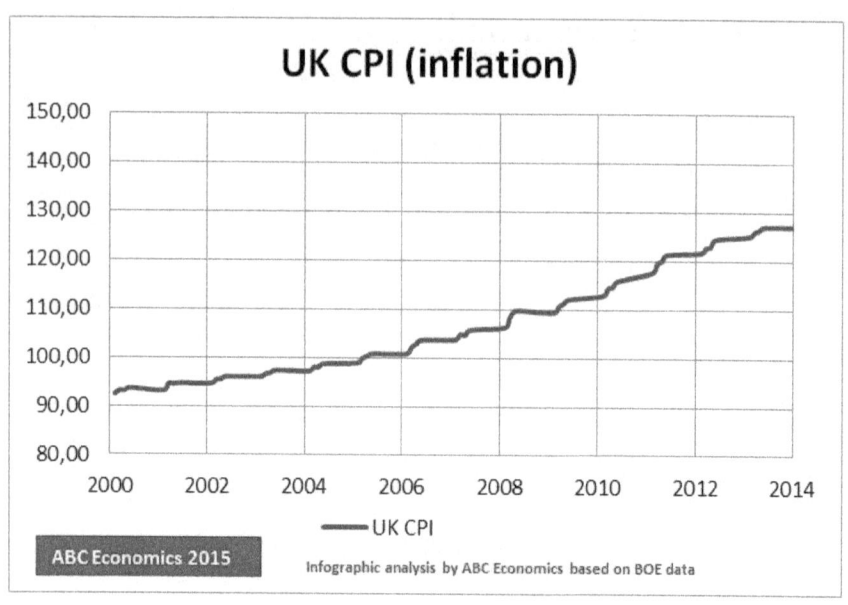
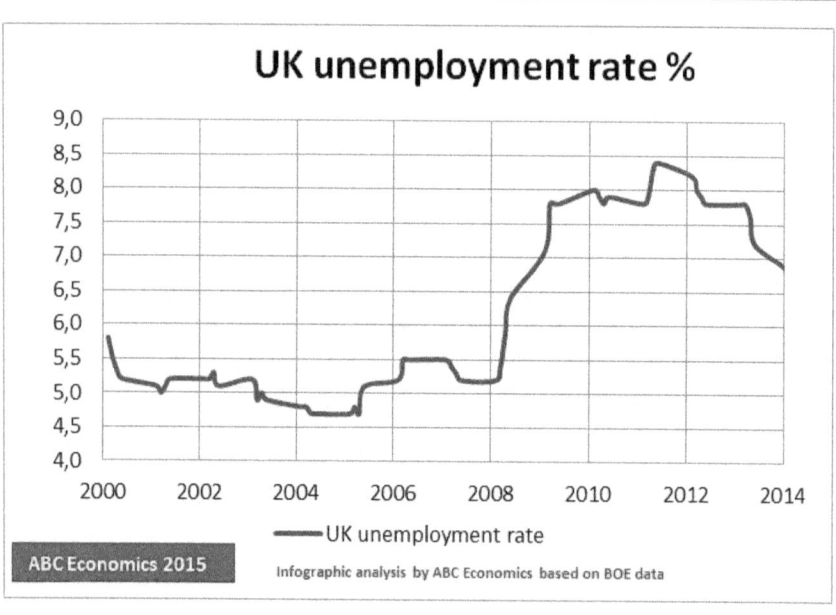

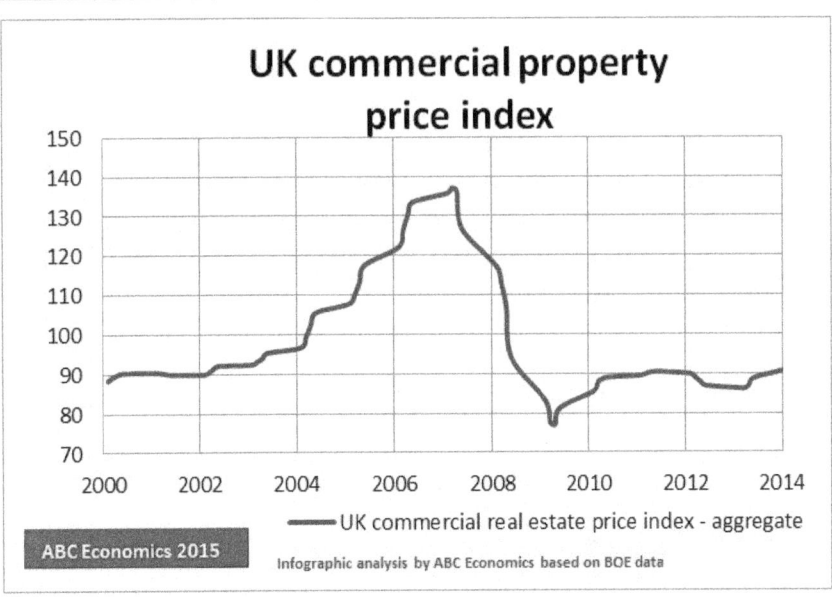

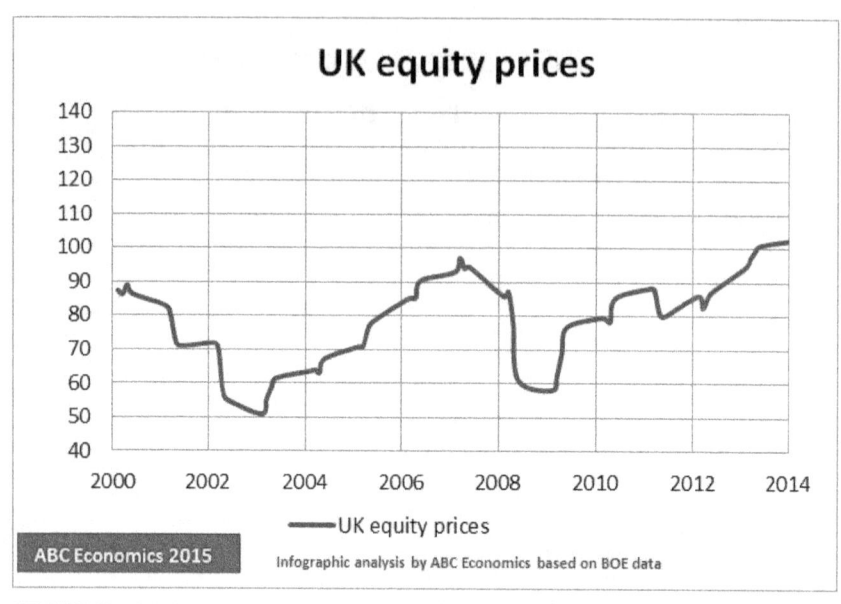
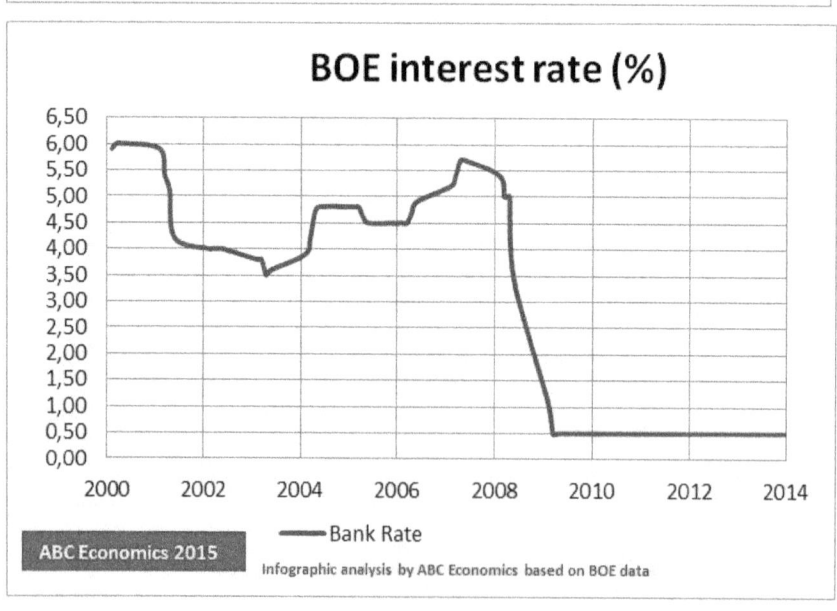

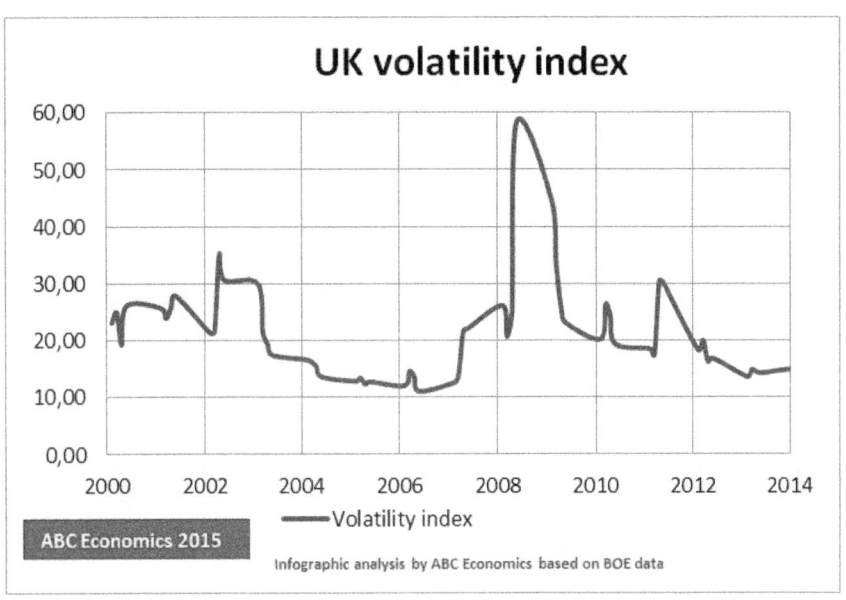

UK economic forecast for 2015-2019

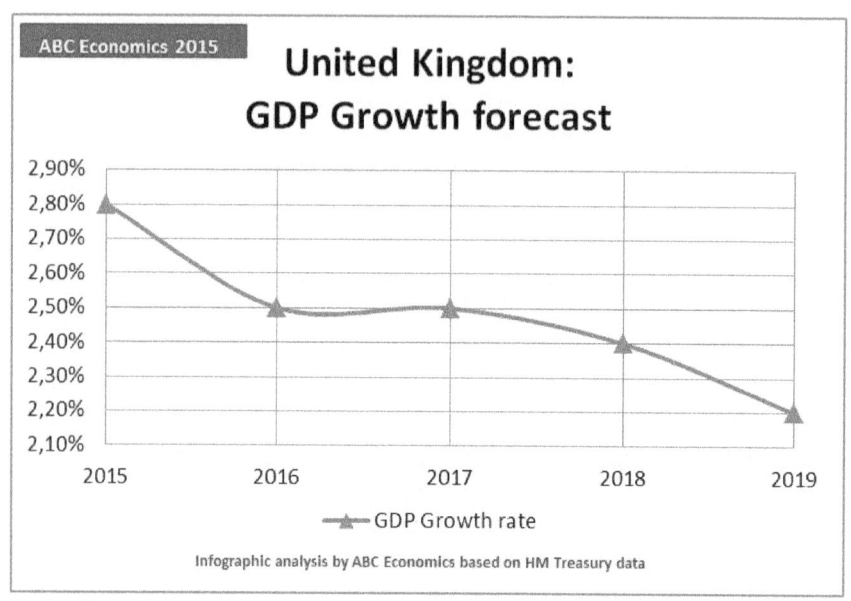

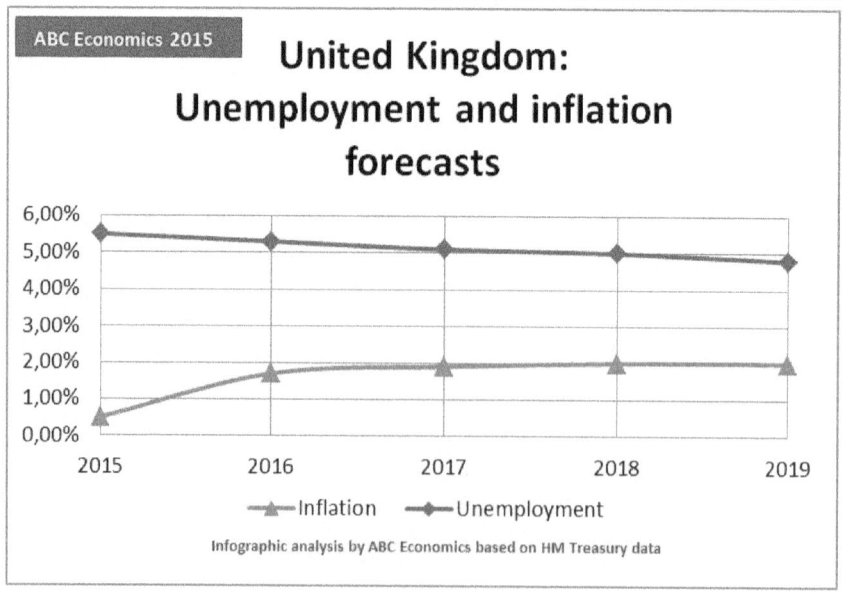

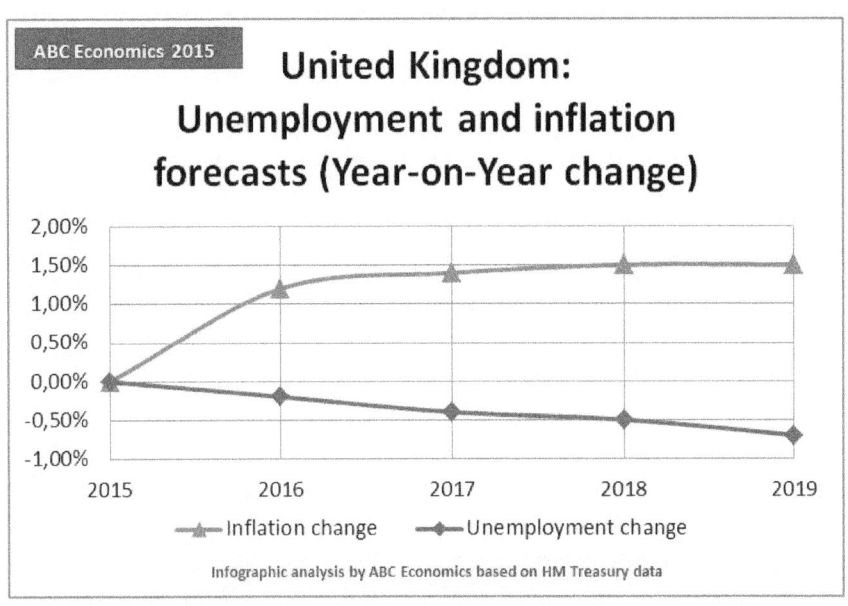
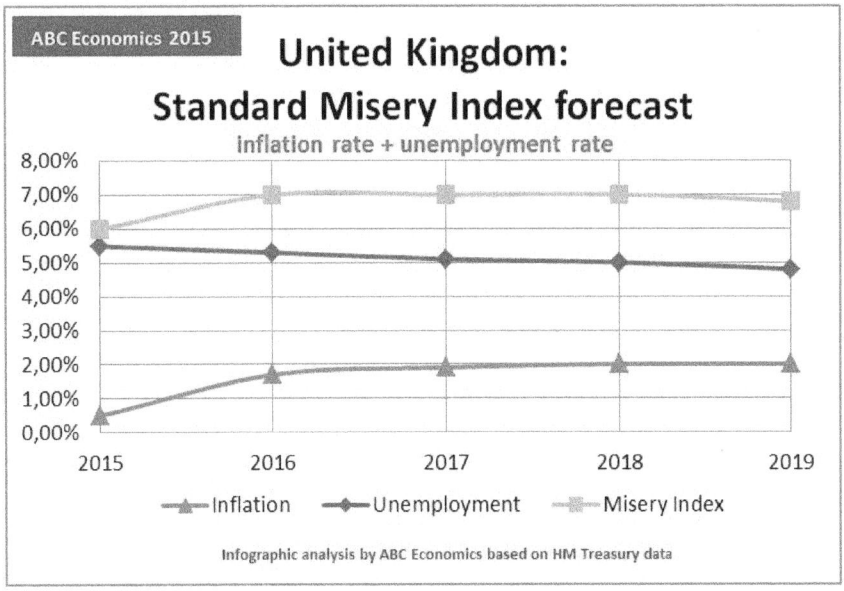

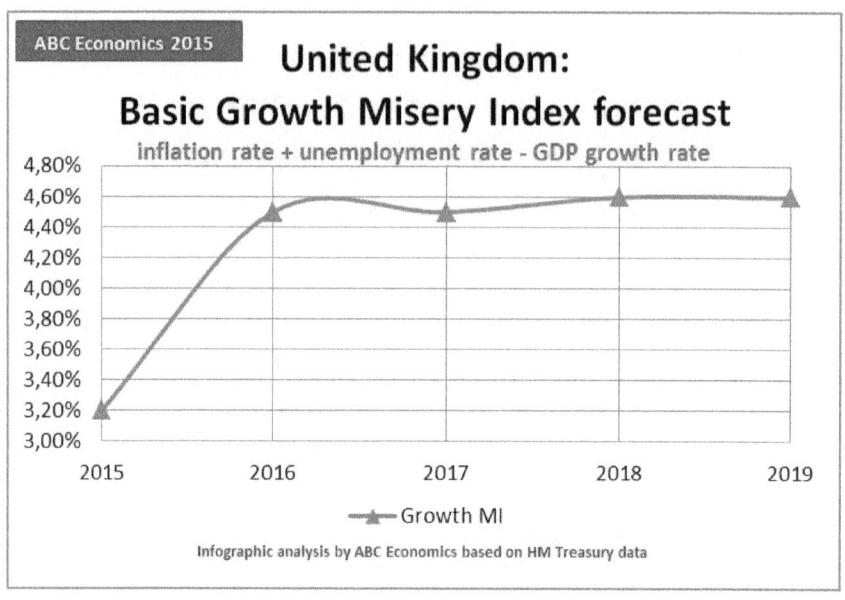

The UK is the EU's main trading partner

The EU is the UK's most important trading partner. According to statistics published by a 2013 House of Commons report, as at 2012 the EU accounted for 46% of its goods and services exports (£224bn) and 51% of its imports (£265bn).

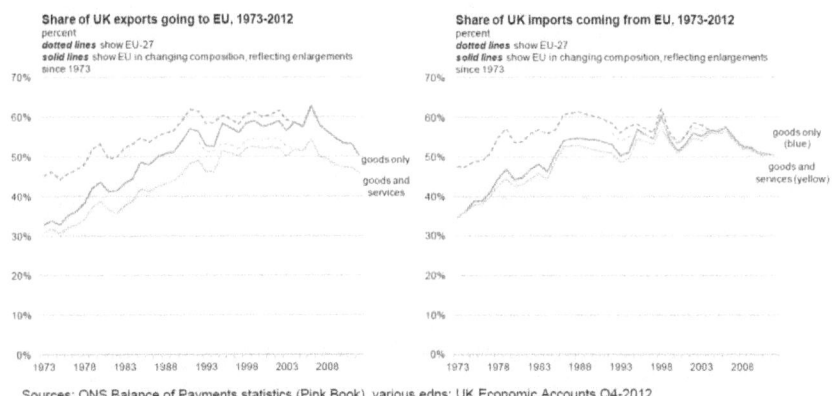

Sources: ONS Balance of Payments statistics (Pink Book), various edns; UK Economic Accounts Q4-2012

From the graphs reported above, the reader will notice a decline in the share of exports going to the EU over the past decade. This is predominantly due to the fact that since 2000 the European Union has signed bilateral commercial deals with Mexico, South Africa, Chile and South Korea, dynamics which "eroded" the UK market-share.

Trade deficits

The UK currently runs an overall trade deficit with the EU. In 2012 the deficit reached £41bn, the highest level since the UK joined the EU in 1980, though as a proportion of GDP, the trade deficit has been larger in the past.

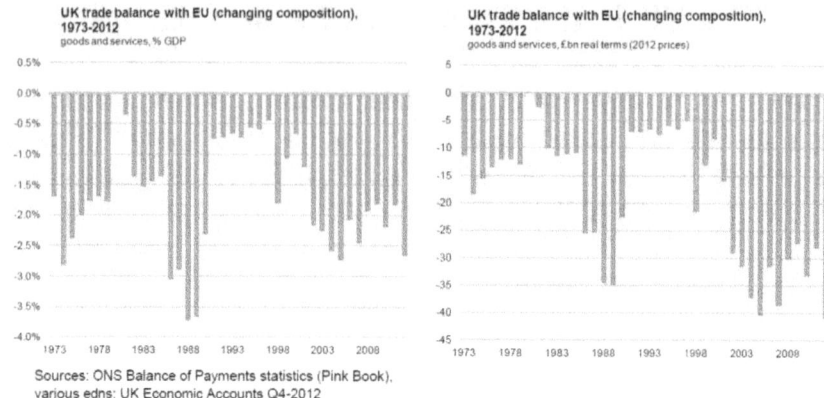

Sources: ONS Balance of Payments statistics (Pink Book), various edns; UK Economic Accounts Q4-2012

More recently, a surplus in financial and business services has partially offset a deficit in goods. As at 2012 the services surplus with the EU was £13bn.

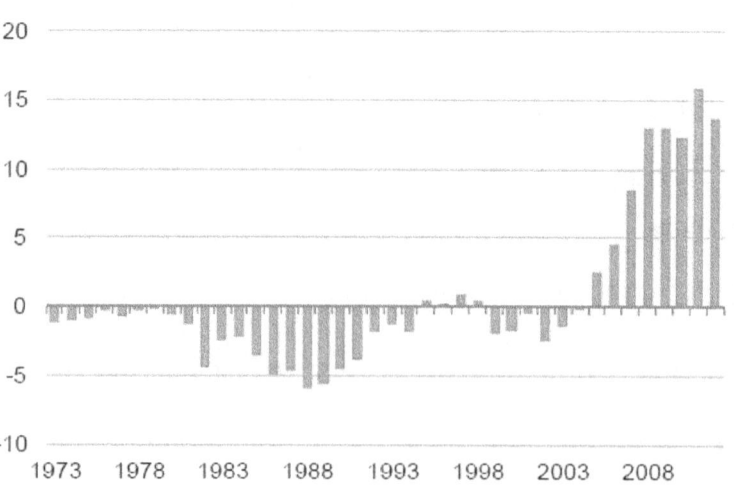

Sources: ONS Balance of Payments statistics (Pink Book), various edns; UK Economic Accounts Q4-2012

SECTION 2:
REASONS TO STAY IN OR LEAVE THE EU

Pro Europa's reasons to stay in the EU

Pro Europa[2] is a think tank supporting in favour of Britain retaining their EU membership. Here their reasons for opposing Brexit.

1. **Jobs**

Around 3.5 million British jobs are directly linked to British membership of the European Union's single market – 1 in 10 British jobs.

2. **Exports & investment**

- The EU buys over 50 per cent of UK exports (54 per cent of goods, 40 per cent of services).
- Over 300,000 British companies and 74 per cent of British exporters operate in other EU markets.
- American and Asian EU firms build factories in Britain because it is in the single market.

3. **Trade**

The EU negotiates trade agreements with the rest of the world. Outside the EU Britain would have to renegotiate trade deals alone. While the EU is the world's largest market, a UK outside the EU would not be a high priority for other counties to negotiate a trade deal.

4. **Consumer clout**

British families enjoy lower mobile phone roaming charges, lower credit card fees, cheaper flights and proper

---

[2] URL: http://proeuropa.org.uk

compensation when flights are delayed or cancelled. These sorts of benefits could not be achieved by Britain alone.

5. Clean environment

Through commonly agreed EU standards, national Governments have achieved improvements to the quality of air, rivers and beaches. Good for Britain and good for Britons holidaying or living abroad!

6. Power to curb the multinationals

The EU has taken on multinational giants like Microsoft, Samsung and Toshiba for unfair competition. The UK would not be able to do this alone.

7. Freedom to work and study abroad – and easy travel

1.4 million British people live abroad in the EU. More than 14,500 UK students took part in the European Union's Erasmus student exchange scheme in 2012-13. Driving licences issued in the UK are valid throughout the EU.

8. Peace and democracy

The EU has helped secure peace among previously warring western European nations. It helped to consolidate democracy in Spain, Portugal, Greece and former Soviet bloc countries and helped preserve peace in the Balkans since the end of the Balkans War. With the UN it now plays a leading role in conflict prevention, peacekeeping and democracy building.

9. Equal pay and non-discrimination

Equal pay for men and women is enshrined in EU law, as are bans on discrimination by age, race or sexual orientation. This benefits Britain and British people who live in other EU countries.

10. Influence in the world

As 28 democracies, and as the world's biggest market, we are strong when we work together. Britain is represented in many international organisations in joint EU delegations – giving Britain more influence than it would have alone. The EU has played a major role in climate, world trade and development.

11. Cutting red tape

Common rules for the common market make it unnecessary to have 28 sets of national regulations.

12. Fighting crime

The European Arrest Warrant replaced long extradition procedures and enables the UK to extradite criminals wanted in other EU countries, and bring to justice criminals wanted in the UK who are hiding in other EU countries.

13. Research funding

The UK is the second largest beneficiary of EU research funds, and the British Government expects future EU research funding to constitute a vital source of income for our world-leading universities and companies.

Daniel Hannan's reasons to leave the EU

Daniel Hannan[3] is the author of 'How we Invented Freedom' (published in the US and Canada as 'Inventing Freedom: how the English-Speaking Peoples Made the Modern World').

1. Since we joined the EEC in 1973, we have been in surplus with every continent in the world except Europe. Over those 27 years, we have run a trade deficit with the other member states that averages out at £30 million per day.

2. In 2010 our gross contribution to the EU budget will be £14 billion. To put this figure in context, all the reductions announced by George Osborne at the Conservative Party Conference would, collectively, save £7 billion a year across the whole of government spending.

3. On the European Commission's own figures, the annual costs of EU regulation outweigh the advantages of the single market by €600 to €180 billion.

4. The Common Agricultural Policy costs every family £1200 a year in higher food bills.

5. Outside the Common Fisheries Policy, Britain could reassert control over its waters out to 200 miles or the median line, which would take in around 65 per cent of North Sea stocks.

6. Successive British governments have refused to say what proportion of domestic laws come from Brussels, but a

---

[3] URL: http://blogs.telegraph.co.uk/news/danielhannan/100020456/ten-reasons-to-leave-the-eu/

thorough analysis by the German Federal Justice Ministry showed that 84 per cent of the legislation in that country came from the EU.

7. Outside the EU, Britain would be free to negotiate much more liberal trade agreements with third countries than is possible under the Common External Tariff.

8. The countries with the highest GDP per capita in Europe are Norway and Switzerland. Both export more, proportionately, to the EU, than Britain does.

9. Outside the EU, Britain could be a deregulated, competitive, offshore haven.

10. Democracy

SECTION 3:
THE LEGAL FRAMEWORK

Brexiting the EU, not leaving Europe. Understanding Article 50 of the Lisbon Treaty

A decision to leave the European Union will begin with the UK Government invoking Article 50 of the Treaty of Lisbon[4] and commence negotiations on the terms of the withdrawal.

Article 50 allows a Member State unilaterally *"to withdraw from the Union in accordance with its own constitutional requirements"* (Article 50, paragraph 1).

> Article 50, paragraph 2:
>
> *A Member State which decides to withdraw shall notify the European Council of its intention. In the light of the guidelines provided by the European Council, the Union shall negotiate and conclude an agreement with that State, setting out the arrangements for its withdrawal, <u>taking account of the framework for its future relationship with the Union</u>. That agreement shall be negotiated in accordance with Article 218(3) of the Treaty on the Functioning of the European Union. It shall be concluded on behalf of the Union by the Council, acting by a qualified majority, after obtaining the consent of the European Parliament.*

> Article 218(3) of the Treaty on the Functioning of the European Union:
>
> *The Commission, or the High Representative of the Union for Foreign Affairs and Security Policy where the agreement envisaged relates exclusively or principally to the common foreign and security policy, shall submit recommendations to*

---

[4] URL: http://www.lisbon-treaty.org/wcm/the-lisbon-treaty/treaty-on-European-union-and-comments/title-6-final-provisions/137-article-50.html

> the Council, which shall adopt a decision authorising the opening of negotiations and, depending on the subject of the agreement envisaged, nominating the Union negotiator or the head of the Union's negotiating team.

While invoking Article 50 of Lisbon, a Member State shall begin negotiations with the European Council i.e. EU Heads of State and Government, particularly with reference to the transitional period whilst *"taking account of the framework for [a State's] future relationship with the Union"* (see Article 50, paragraph 2).

According to Sir David Edward, a former high profile judge at the European Court of Justice from 1992 to 2004, a long negotiation period under Article 50 would be necessary because *"withdrawal from the Union would involve the unravelling of a highly complex skein of budgetary, legal, political, financial, commercial and personal relationships, liabilities and obligations"*. However, it should be noted that (i) negotiations are expected to last a maximum of two years (unless extended by unanimous agreement) and (ii) the decision to leave does not require formal agreement of the other Member States as withdrawal can happen, whether or not there is a withdrawal agreement, two years after the leaving State notifies the European Council of its intention to leave the EU.

> Article 50, paragraph 3:
>
> *The Treaties shall cease to apply to the State in question from the date of entry into force of the withdrawal agreement or, failing that, two years after the notification referred to in paragraph 2, unless the European Council, in agreement with the Member State concerned, unanimously decides to extend this period.*

Under paragraph 5 of Article 50, if a State which has withdrawn from the Union asks to re-join, it must re-apply under the procedure referred to in Article 49 that implies that the applicant would start completely afresh.

> Article 49:
>
> *Any European State which respects the values referred to in Article 2 and is committed to promoting them may apply to become a member of the Union. The European Parliament and national Parliaments shall be notified of this application. The applicant State shall address its application to the Council, which shall act unanimously after consulting the Commission and after receiving the assent of the European Parliament, which shall act by an absolute majority of its component members. The conditions of admission and the adjustments to the Treaties on which the Union is founded, which such admission entails, shall be the subject of an agreement between the Member States and the applicant State. This agreement shall be submitted for ratification by all the contracting States in accordance with their respective constitutional requirements. The conditions of eligibility agreed upon by the European Council shall be taken into account.*

As noted by Adam Łazowski, a prominent law academic at the University of Westminster, Brexit could require the revision or renegotiation of three treaties: one to allow the departing State to withdraw; another to amend the EU Treaties to remove references to the departing State; and possibly a third to allow the departing State to join EFTA and remain in the EEA.

According to Lazowski: *"unlike accession treaties, withdrawal agreements do not form part of EU primary law. Thus, unless a special formula is developed, they cannot amend the treaties on which the EU is based. This implies that alongside an international treaty regulating withdrawal, the remaining member states would have to negotiate between themselves a treaty amending the founding treaties in order to repeal all provisions touching upon the departing country"*.

Additionally, Lazowski notes that *"further complexities may be added if a departing country chooses to make a rapid move from the EU to the European Economic Area (EEA) instead. That would necessitate a third treaty regulating the terms of accession to EFTA and a fourth to deal with the accession to the EEA. The latter would require the approval of the EU and its member states, the EEA-EFTA countries and the departing/joining country"*.

Alternatives to EU membership: EFTA and EEA

This chapter was largely compiled by editing material originally published on the official web portal of the EFTA (http://www.efta.int/).

Having described the legal framework around Brexit, we now turn our attention to the most likely alternatives to the EU: the European Free Trade Area (EFTA) and the European Economic Area (EEA).

European Free Trade Area (EFTA)

EFTA was founded by the Stockholm Convention in 1960. The immediate aim of the Association was to provide a framework for the liberalisation of trade in goods amongst its Member States. At the same time, EFTA was established as an economic counterbalance to the more politically driven European Economic Community (EEC). Relations with the EEC, later the European Community (EC) and the European Union (EU), have been at the core of EFTA activities from the beginning. In the 1970s, the EFTA States concluded free trade agreements with the EC; in 1994 the EEA Agreement entered into force. Since the beginning of the 1990s, EFTA has actively pursued trade relations with third countries in and beyond Europe. The first partners were the Central and Eastern European countries, followed by the countries in the Mediterranean area. In recent years, EFTA's network of free trade agreements has reached across the Atlantic as well as into Asia.

EFTA was founded by the following seven countries: Austria, Denmark, Norway, Portugal, Sweden, Switzerland and the United Kingdom. Finland joined in 1961, Iceland in 1970 and

Liechtenstein in 1991. In 1973, the United Kingdom and Denmark left EFTA to join the EC. They were followed by Portugal in 1986 and by Austria, Finland and Sweden in 1995. Today the EFTA Member States are Iceland, Liechtenstein, Norway and Switzerland.

The Association is responsible for the management of:

- The EFTA Convention, which forms the legal basis of the organisation and governs free trade relations between the EFTA States;
- EFTA's worldwide network of free trade and partnership agreements; and
- The European Economic Area (EEA) Agreement, which enables three of the four EFTA Member States (Iceland, Liechtenstein and Norway) to participate in the EU's Internal Market.

European Economic Area (EEA)

Signed in 1992 and operational from 1994, the Agreement on the European Economic Area (EEA), which entered into force on 1 January 1994, brings together the EU Member States and the three EEA EFTA States — Iceland, Liechtenstein and Norway — in a single market, referred to as the "Internal Market".

The EEA Agreement states that when a country becomes a member of the European Union, it shall also apply to become party to the EEA Agreement (Article 128), thus leading to an enlargement of the EEA.

The EEA Agreement provides for the inclusion of EU legislation covering the four freedoms — the free movement of goods, services, persons and capital — throughout the 31 EEA States. In addition, the Agreement covers cooperation in other important areas such as research and development, education, social policy, the environment, consumer protection, tourism and culture, collectively known as "flanking and horizontal" policies. The Agreement guarantees equal rights and obligations within the Internal Market for citizens and economic operators in the EEA.

What is the EEA Not?

The EEA Agreement does not cover the following EU policies:

- Common Agriculture and Fisheries Policies (although the Agreement contains provisions on various aspects of trade in agricultural and fish products);
- Customs Union;
- Common Trade Policy;
- Common Foreign and Security Policy;
- Justice and Home Affairs (even though the EFTA countries are part of the Schengen area); or
- Monetary Union (EMU).

Switzerland is not part of the EEA Agreement, but has a bilateral agreement with the EU.

Advantages of joining EFTA

A study by René Schwok and Cenni Najy, respectively a Professor and a researcher at the University of Geneva, identified some of the advantages arising from the UK joining EFTA:

- a far lower UK financial contribution, which would exclude the CAP;
- the UK Government would be free to set its VAT level;
- capacity to ratify free-trade agreements faster and with more partners than the EU and greater freedom of manoeuvre to sign free trade agreements worldwide;
- UK bilateral agreements with the EU would better protect British sovereignty, notwithstanding a loss of influence

In addition to a number of potential side-effects, namely:

- Joining EFTA could entail a difficult application process with possibility of veto from existing Member(s);
- EFTA a homogenous bloc in terms of countries' size, economic development and trade preferences. UK might not fit in or might change the dynamic of the group to the disadvantage of existing members.

The reader should note that it is not possible to become a party to the EEA Agreement without being a member of either the EU or EFTA, so the UK would have to re-join EFTA if it left the EU in order to remain in the EEA. Three has also been a suggestion that Article 127 of the EEA Agreement might allow continued free trade and movement between a withdrawing state and the EEA for 12 months after a Member State signals its withdrawal.

EU-exit without a free trade agreement

Extract from the House of Commons Library, Research Paper No. 13/42

Were it to leave, the UK's trading relationship with the EU would be the product of negotiation. A vast number of different arrangements could result, but for the purposes of analysis, considering a situation in which the UK negotiates no preferential market access with the EU offers a clearly defined point of reference. In this instance, the terms of World Trade Organisation (WTO) membership limit the range of outcomes. The details of such an arrangement are discussed below.

Tariff barriers

The principle of non-discrimination requires WTO members not to treat any member less advantageously than any other: grant one country preferential treatment, and the same must be done for everyone else. There are exceptions for regional free trade areas and customs unions like the EU, but the principle implies that, outside of these, the tariff that applies to the **'most-favoured nation' (MFN)** must similarly apply to all.

In practice, this would prevent discriminatory or punitive tariffs being levied by either the EU on the UK, or vice versa. The maximum tariff would be that applied to the MFN. As the chart shows, the EU's MFN tariff has fallen over time, meaning that in this particular context the 'advantage' of membership has declined. However, given that MFN tariffs would be imposed on around 90% of the UK's goods exports to the EU by value, it would necessarily mean many exporters becoming less price competitive, to varying degrees, than their counterparts operating within the remaining EU, and those within countries with which the EU has preferential trading relationships. Similarly, because the UK has negotiated as part of the EU at the WTO, it is likely that it would inherit the EU's tariff regime at the time of leaving, meaning, at least initially, higher prices would be faced by consumers buying imports from the EU and those countries with which the EU has trade agreements.

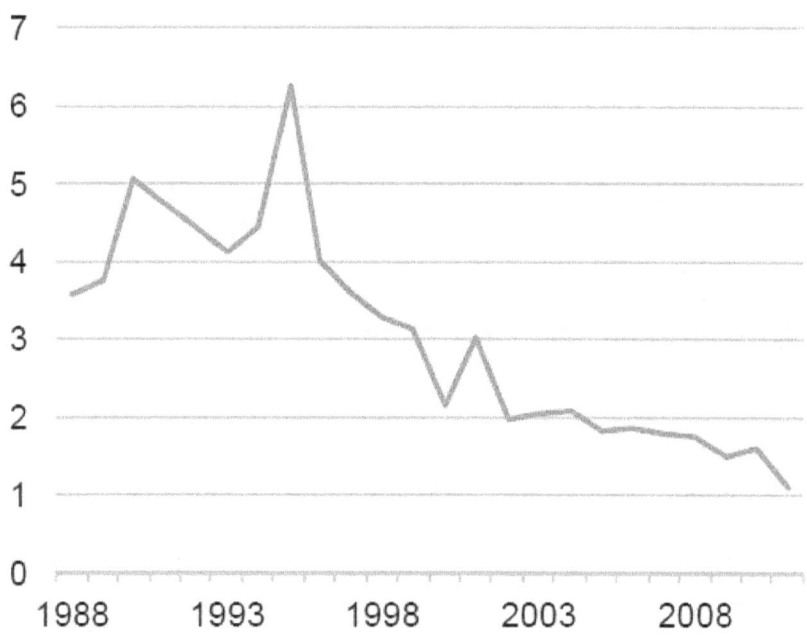

EU average (trade-weighted) MFN tariff
percent, 1988-2011

Source: data.worldbank.org

The implications of a move to an MFN trading arrangement for exporters and domestic consumers would vary considerably by sector, as illustrated in the chart below, which compares the EU's average MFN tariff across over 1,200 product groups with the UK's trade balance in each. The size of the bubbles represents total trade in the commodity (imports plus exports). For instance, without a trade agreement, a tariff of 4.1% would be applied to liquefied natural gas exports from the UK to the EU; a tariff of 12.8% to wheat and meslin; and a tariff of 6% to unwrought aluminium, all items which the UK currently runs a trade surplus with the EU. UK consumers would face higher prices, although the precise effects would depend on how the Government altered the tariff structure it 'inherited' on leaving the EU. Without any change, a 32% tariff would be levied on imports of wine, for instance, and a 9.8% tariff on motor vehicles.

Non-tariff barriers

Non-tariff barriers to trade refer to a range of measures that have the effect of reducing imports, either intentionally or unintentionally. They include anti-dumping measures that prevent goods being exported at a price below production cost (usually by the application of an additional duty), and product standards, such as labelling, packaging and sanitary requirements. Support to domestic producers and export subsidies, such as those provided under the Common Agricultural Policy (CAP), can also be interpreted as non-tariff barriers since they inhibit market access by foreign producers on equal terms. In the context of falling tariff barriers, such non-tariff measures have become more widely used as a means to protect domestic producers from foreign competition.

The terms of WTO agreements limit the circumstances in which such measures can be applied, and in particular uphold the principle of non-discrimination that would prohibit punitive measures against the UK were it to leave. Nonetheless, the EU has provisional or definitive anti-dumping tariffs in place against more than a hundred other products in 24 countries; recently, its imposition of tariffs on Chinese solar panels has raised fears that retaliatory measures by China will spark a 'trade war'.

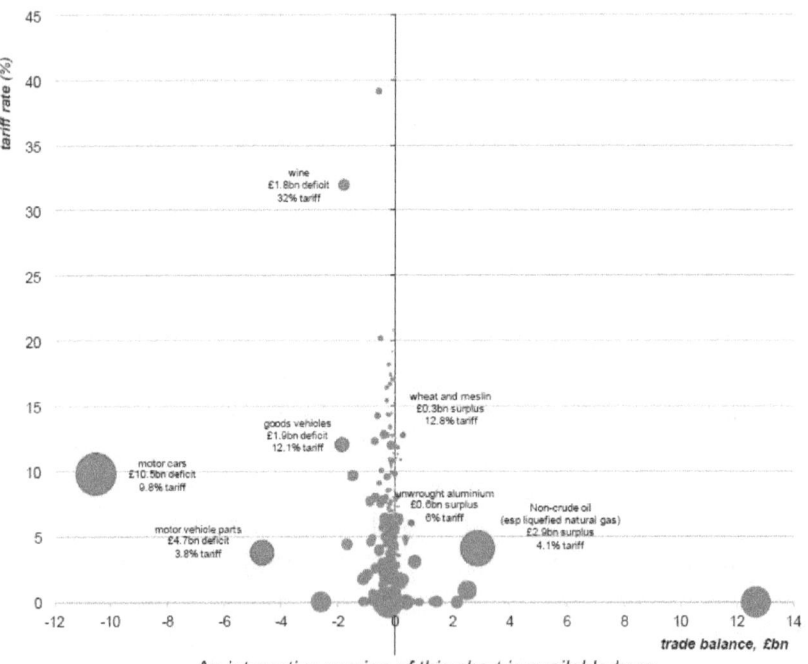

EU MFN tariff (vertical axis) vs UK-EU trade bance (horizontal axis), 2011
HS4 product categories; bubble size represents total value of trade (imports plus exports)

An interactive version of this chart is available here

Just as important in a trade context, however, are the standards required of products imported from outside the EU. All UK businesses must comply with these standards already, although as in other areas of regulation, withdrawal raises the prospect of costly divergences between the UK and EU product standards. On the other hand, some proponents of withdrawal argue that, were it to leave the both EU and the single market, only exporters would have to be bound by the EU's product standards, leaving other businesses free to operate under a UK regime.

Services trade

Without further negotiation, the UK's trade in services with the EU would be governed by the WTO General Agreement on Trade in Services (GATS). Under this agreement, EU Member States (and other parties to the agreement) have chosen which sectors they are prepared to liberalise, and the time scale over which they wish to do so. As with trade in goods, GATS also operates on the principle of non-discrimination, meaning broadly that outside preferential agreements, restrictions on market access must be applied uniformly across all countries.

Barriers to services trade are usually in the form of non-tariff barriers, such as domestic laws and regulations, also known as 'behind the border' measures. In general, services markets are more highly regulated than the market for goods. Often, regulation is intended to meet social objectives, or to correct failures in supply, rather than directly to restrict foreign suppliers, but the effect on market access for foreign companies can in some cases be highly restrictive. EU Member States retain considerable national discretion over services regulation and supervision. Just as a fully level playing field in services trade does not exist within the EU, so exporters from outside the EU face different levels of market access in individual Member States. However, the level of market access would generally be far more limited for UK exporters under a GATS arrangement than it is currently for a number of reasons:

- many restrictions that are forbidden within the EU remain applicable to firms outside the EU because Member States have made no commitments under the GATS schedules in those areas;
- the right of commercial establishment is guaranteed under EU treaties, significantly facilitating trade in services provided via the commercial presence of a foreign firm;
- the free movement of labour significantly facilitates trade in services provided through the presence of people in the territory of another economy;
- EU competition policy prevents, to an extent, barriers to services trade arising from incumbent firms benefitting from excessive market power;
- the Treaty rights with respect to free movement of services, freedom of establishment, and free movement of labour are enforced supranationally by the EU Court of Justice, underpinned by extensive case law on services exchange. Under GATS, an independent panel can be appointed to settle and enforce disputes, but there is no presumed right of market access; the job of the panel is merely to assess whether the barrier in question non-discriminatory.

As well as affecting cross-border trade in services, these restrictions could also have implications for UK companies providing services through a commercial presence (effectively outward direct investment) in other Member States. The EU Treaties require that a service provider from one Member State be legally free to establish in another, while continuing to be regulated by the authorities of its home country. A UK company that provides services through establishments in other Member States may find, if the UK is no longer a member of the EU, that it has to comply with the requirements of a foreign regulatory authority.

EU-exit under a negotiated arrangement

Extract from the House of Commons Library, Research Paper No. 13/42

Beyond the MFN position, there are a host of more preferential trade arrangements between the EU and UK that may be negotiated, although there is likely to be a trade-off between the level of access to the single market (i.e. freedom from tariff and non-tariff barriers to trade), and freedom from EU product regulations, social and employment legislation, and budgetary contributions.

Under a 'Swiss' or an EEA model, assuming such an arrangement could be negotiated, the restrictions on trade outlined above would be significantly reduced. In particular, the EEA has full, tariff-free access to the internal market, and the EU's 'four freedoms' concerning movement of goods, services, capital and labour, apply equally to Norway, Iceland and Liechtenstein as they do to full Member States. However, relative to a position of full Membership, a number of restrictions on trade would still apply under an EEA or 'Swiss' approach. These are discussed below.

Rules of origin

Because the EU operates with a common external tariff, goods entering from outside can travel freely within the Union once that tariff has been paid (e.g. a mobile phone imported into the UK from China can be re-exported to the rest of the EU tariff free). The same is not true of goods that enter the EU via the EEA (e.g. a mobile phone from China re-exported to the EU from Norway) or via other countries with which the EU has a free or preferential trading relationship, because they do not share the EU's common external tariff. Determining where a good originated, and hence whether it should attract tariffs, is done through the EU's Rules of Origin. Given the complexity of some global supply chains and the range of preferential trading relationships the EU operates, this can be a difficult, time-consuming and often subjective process.60 Some of this burden, according to the Trade Policy Research Centre, would fall on UK firms in the form of administrative and compliance costs; they note that "the process of adapting to rules of origin-based duty-free trade under a new UK-EU free trade agreement would be tedious, costly and disruptive to trade".

In its briefing on Rules of Origin, the US Congressional Research Service also noted that satisfying their requirements could be costly for businesses:

The benefit conferred by the preferential schemes in certain cases becomes marginal in comparison with the administrative workload and cost to plan the product mix to comply with the preferential ROO. This often leads to instances where firms, although meeting the necessary conditions for origin, decide that it is simpler and cheaper to pay the MFN tariff rates.

The briefing cites a 1992 study in connection with the EC-EFTA agreement that found that the cost of border formalities to determine the origin of products amounted to at least 3% of the value of the goods concerned.61

Anti-dumping and other non-tariff barriers

Were the UK in the EEA or adopted the Swiss model, goods would still be susceptible to anti-dumping action by the EU; for instance, in 2005, the EU imposed a 16% duty on

Norwegian salmon. As discussed in Chapter 4, membership of the EEA or the negotiation of bilateral agreements analogous to those in Switzerland would also require the UK to adopt EU product standards (and other regulations) across the whole economy.

Restrictions on services trade

As part of the EU's internal market, EEA countries like Norway are able to conduct services trade on the same basis as other Member States. However, as in other areas, they lack direct influence over how services are regulated at EU level. The loss of influence over the regulatory agenda and the ability to push directly for further services trade liberalisation may be particularly important for the UK, given that it has a comparative advantage in a number of sectors, and runs a services trade surplus with the EU. Many voices in the financial services industry believe that the UK's ongoing influence over the regulatory agenda is important, particularly as the eurozone crisis brings about a wave of euro area-specific regulation and reform that could be potentially discriminatory to the City. In evidence to the Foreign Affairs Committee, TheCityUK, the lobbying body for the financial services industry, wrote:

... the provision of financial services in the UK by non-UK firms has become to a large degree dependent on the maintenance of [a] common EU legal framework and the UK's part in devising it and operating within it. The evolutionary character of this common legal framework means that the UK must be engaged at all levels of policy development.

An example of such regulation is the effort by the European Central Bank (ECB), backed by France and Germany, to require clearing houses that deal in significant volumes of euro-denominated transactions to be located within the euro area; the UK Government is currently challenging these proposals at the European Court of Justice on the grounds that they contravene the single market principles of free movement of services and capital across the Union. On the other hand, sceptics might point out that the very fact that the UK failed to secure concessions for its financial services industry, despite demanding them at the December 2011 Council summit at which it eventually wielded its 'veto', illustrates its powerlessness to influence the agenda even within the EU.

Were it to leave both the EU and the EEA, in negotiating a trade relationship with the EU, the UK may face particular difficulties, firstly in securing ongoing access to services markets, and secondly in ensuring it benefits from further liberalisation of trade in services within the EU. For instance, despite extensive negotiations on the matter, there is no general and encompassing agreement on the free movement of services between the EU and Switzerland. Financial services trade is an area that could be particularly affected by a 'Swiss' approach.

SECTION 4:
THE ECONOMIC IMPACT OF BREXIT

Brexit: would independence over trade policy lead to better results?

Extract from the House of Commons Library, Research Paper No. 13/42

It is often suggested that independence over trade policy would allow the UK to join other free trade areas, such as NAFTA and forge its own bilateral free trade agreements that are tailored to its particular economic circumstances; as part of the EU, this is legally impossible. This freedom, it is argued, would allow the UK to refocus its trade on economies with brighter prospects and rectify its persistent trade deficit.

It is open to debate whether the UK's capacity to export to the rest of the world, and particularly to high growth emerging economies, is significantly held back by EU membership. Trade between the UK on the one hand, and China and India on the other, has more than doubled since 2006, while the share of exports going to the EU has declined from 54% to 46%. Germany, meanwhile, exported four times more to China than the UK does by value, and came close to a current account balance with it in 2012. Even outside the EU, the structure and orientation of the UK economy are likely to place important constraints on its capacity to re-orientate its trade in the medium-term.

From a British perspective, the EU's trade policy does not appear to be wholly misguided in geographical terms; most of the countries with which the EU is currently negotiating an FTA are among the UK's top trading partners.

Some have noted that the EU has less interest in pursuing free trade agreements with Commonwealth countries than the UK: at 9.5%, the UK's export share to the Commonwealth is greater than, for instance, France's (5.7%) or Germany's (5.0%). The EU already has preferential trading arrangements with 16 of the 53 other Commonwealth members, covering around a third of the UK's total Commonwealth exports, and is in negotiations with a further 26, covering an additional 45%; notable exceptions include Australia and Pakistan.

The EU has thus far failed to secure any preferential trade agreements with Brazil, India or China, but whether the UK's trade negotiating strength and efficiency would be greater outside the EU is uncertain.

On the one hand, concluding deals might be easier for the UK alone, given the greater diversity of interests involved when the EU negotiates as a group; on the other, the smaller size of its market may mean deals with the EU, like the Transatlantic Trade and Investment Partnership (the proposed FTA with the United States) are afforded greater priority by non-EU countries than deals with the UK alone. Typically, the EFTA countries follow in the EU's path when it comes to FTA negotiation (i.e. agreements are reached with the EEA and EFTA shortly after those with the EU), although in the case of the recent South Korea FTA, EFTA led the way.

A particular area where UK interests may be poorly represented in EU trade negotiations is services market access.

Language, time zone and structural features of the UK economy give it a comparative advantage in cross-border services trade, but, according to Open Europe, *"the EU's lack of domestic liberalisation in services trade limits the enthusiasm of member states to push and prioritise these issues with third countries".*

The recent exclusion of audio-visual services from the US free-trade negotiations, following pressure from France, is an example of the sensitivities attached to this area of trade liberalisation and the compromises that must be struck when 28 countries negotiate as a group.

Securing free trade with EU after Brexit. Easy wins and challenges

Open Europe's assessment of how withdrawal from the EU would impact eight of the UK's key exporting industries, in both the goods and services sectors.

EU regulation now covers most parts of the UK economy, including the public sector, which is largely non-tradable, and other domestic firms which do not export. This means that Brexit – for better or worse – would have an impact across the entire UK economy. In this briefing, however, we focus on the impact of EU withdrawal on exports of UK goods and services, which account for 30% of UK GDP (the EU accounts for 44% of the UK's total exports).

The sectors analysed by Open Europe account for 53% of the UK's global exports and 47% of its exports to the EU. Mineral fuels (such as crude oil) and miscellaneous manufactured goods make up the majority of other UK exports to the EU not assessed in the briefing.

Outside of the EU, there are two major potential benefits for the UK:

- The ability to pursue lighter and more tailored regulation not possible under EU membership.
- The ability to strike new trade deals with the rest of the world not possible in a club of 28 members.

Key findings: Initial impact of Brexit on UK exporting industries

All the exporting sectors assessed – cars; chemicals and pharmaceuticals; aerospace; capital goods and machinery; food, beverages and tobacco; financial services; insurance; and professional services – would experience initial disruption and uncertainty in the event of Brexit.

The 35% of the UK's goods exports to the EU that could be subject to high tariffs (above 4%) upon exit – in sectors such as cars, chemicals and food – and the highly regulated financial services sector would be particularly vulnerable to initial disruption.

Initial impact of Brexit?

	Sector	% exported to EU	Trade deficit/ Surplus with EU (£bn)	Potential barriers to EU markets	Risk of disruption	Chances of similar EU access	Possible conditions attached
Goods	Cars	35.0	-13.95	10% tariff	High	High	Basic standards
	Chemicals	56.6	-7.82	4.6% tariff	High	Medium to high	Adhering to EU's regulatory standards
	Aerospace	44.6	2.56	Zero tariffs	High	High	Basic standards
	Machinery	30.7	-5.47	1.7% to 4.5% tariffs	Medium	High	Basic standards
	Food, Beverages & Tobacco	60.5	-16.56	Average tariffs over 20% and higher	High	Medium to high	Keep external tariff with rules on foreign content
Services	Financial services	41.4	16.06	Various EU market access regulations	High	Low	Equivalent regulation; possibly still with patchy access
	Insurance	18.4	3.85	Various EU market access regulations	Medium	Medium	Equivalent regulation; possibly still with patchy access
	Professional services	29.8	-1.92	Primarily national market access regulations	Medium	Medium	Mutual recognition, free movement of professionals

However, in a UK and EU exit negotiation there is a high likelihood that the UK and the EU could conclude preferential trade deals covering the five goods sectors assessed by Open Europe. In all these sectors UK firms would face new administration costs at the EU border, due to rules governing foreign content in their products. In the case of chemicals and food, a deal would potentially come with strict conditions such as adhering to the EU's high regulatory costs or maintaining tariffs with the rest of the world to the cost of UK consumers – negating some of the potential benefits of Brexit.

For the remaining services sectors, and financial services in particular, guaranteeing seamless access to EU markets for UK businesses will be more difficult, not least because the UK has a deficit with the EU in goods, but a surplus in services.

All sectors would suffer from the UK's loss of voting rights in the EU, but for industries such as the financial sector the impact could be greater since the barriers to entering European markets could be increased by new EU regulations over which the UK has no votes.

Trade and Welfare effects of leaving the EU

Below the Centre for Economic Performance (CEP) paper on the effects of Brexit on the UK economy.

Points to note

- Over half of all UK exports go to the rest of the European Union (EU) – this corresponds to almost 15% of national income (GDP).
- One cost of the UK leaving the EU ('Brexit') would be less trade with the EU because of higher tariff and non-tariff barriers today and reduced benefits from lower trade costs in the future. A benefit of leaving would be a lower net fiscal contribution.
- We consider a pessimistic scenario where the UK suffers some formal increase in trade costs compared with an optimistic one where it does not. A conventional calculation from a quantitative trade model produces income losses of around 3.1% of GDP (£50 billion) in the pessimistic case or 1.1% in the optimistic case (£18 billion).
- When we factor in more realistic dynamic losses from lower productivity growth, a conservative estimate would double losses to 2.2% of GDP even in the most optimistic case. In the pessimistic case, there would be income falls of 6.3% to 9.5% of GDP, a loss of a similar size to that resulting from the global financial crisis of 2008/09.
- There are further effects on immigration, foreign investment and regulations. Although harder to quantify,

Brexit is also likely, on balance, to depress income through these channels.
- Our current assessment is that leaving the EU would be likely to impose substantial costs on the UK economy and would be a very risky gamble.

Introduction

Since a speech by the Prime Minister in January 2013, the Conservative party has been committed to holding a referendum on the UK's membership of the European Union (EU) in 2017. So this is a good moment to consider what would be the likely economic effects on the UK from such a move (commonly called 'Brexit').

Eurosceptics emphasise greater national sovereignty from Brexit while Europhiles tend to focus on the importance of ever greater unity to reduce the risks of the political conflicts that ravaged Europe in the first half of the twentieth century. These are important matters, but this analysis focuses on the more mundane (but quantifiable) economic issues, especially trade.

Trade with the EU has increased substantially over the last four decades since the UK joined.

Just over 30% of UK exports went to the EU in 1973, but this has risen to over half today (55% in 2008). This is an impressive figure as the rest of the EU only accounts for a fifth of global GDP. Given that the UK government is trying to rebalance the economy towards export-based growth, the 15% of GDP destined for the EU is a significant share.

The UK transfers some resources to the EU, mainly to subsidise agriculture and poorer members. Abstracting from transition costs and any direct or indirect benefit to the UK from these fiscal transfers, leaving the EU would bring home the equivalent of about 0.53% of national income (HM Treasury, 2013). This is argued to be the main potential benefit of Brexit.

The main potential cost would be in the form of lower trade, so we focus on this. There are also costs and benefits that are harder to quantify relating to regulations, immigration and foreign direct investment, which we discuss more briefly.

Conventional static costs and benefits: overview

We use a state-of-the-art quantitative model of international trade to calculate the impact on the welfare of the UK population of leaving the EU. Full details are provided in a companion technical paper (Ottaviano et al, 2014). The model takes account of trade in 35 sectors (including intermediates) among the 40 major countries in the world.

Like just about all other quantitative trade models, this is a conventional static approach and the gains from trade are primarily due to countries specialising in their area of comparative advantage. It does not take account of dynamic effects of trade on productivity growth or other static effects of trade on competition, scale and product variety. It thus underestimates the welfare gains from remaining in the EU.

Although there is no standard quantifiable model of such dynamic gains, we estimate some rough magnitudes later on.

To quantify the changes, we need to make some assumptions about how trade costs will change between the UK and the EU in the event of Brexit. We consider two scenarios. The 'optimistic' view is that the UK would continue to enjoy the same amount of access to the EU's internal market as it currently does, much like Switzerland and Norway (which are members of the European Free Trade Association, EFTA). Most commentators, however, believe that, as a large ex-member, the UK would not be able to negotiate such favourable terms. Hence, we also consider a 'pessimistic' scenario where there are increases in trade costs.

There are three possible reasons why trade costs may increase after Brexit:

- Higher tariff barriers between the UK and the EU.
- Higher non-tariff barriers to trade (arising from different regulations, border controls, etc.) between the UK and the EU.
- The UK will not participate in future steps that the EU takes towards deeper integration reducing non-tariff barriers.

In our pessimistic scenario, we assume that MFN tariffs on goods will apply to UK-EU trade.

This seems reasonable immediately following withdrawal, but some argue that the UK may be able to negotiate a better tariff deal in the medium term. Hence, in our optimistic scenario, we assume tariffs continue to be zero.

Another important source of trade costs lies in non-tariff barriers related to regulations and other legal obstacles that affect not only goods but also services. In our optimistic scenario, we assume that the UK would face one quarter of the reducible cost of non-tariff barriers faced by the United States, while in our pessimistic scenario, we assume that the UK would face as much as two thirds.

Finally, intra-EU trade costs have been steadily falling over time, approximately 40% faster than in other OECD countries. From the perspective of a decade from now, non-tariff barriers inside the EU could be relatively smaller. In our pessimistic scenario, we assume that intra-EU non-tariff barriers continue to fall 40% faster than in the rest of the world, leading to a cumulative fall in trade costs of 10%, a benefit that the UK would lose in the case of an exit.

In our optimistic scenario, we assume that intra-EU barriers fall only 20% faster than in the rest of the world, leading to a total fall in trade costs of only 5.7%, meaning that the UK would lose less after an exit.

Conventional static costs and benefits: details

The table below shows the results from our static trade model. In the optimistic scenario, there is an overall welfare loss of 1.13% driven by current and future changes in non-tariff barriers.

These are not trivial because such barriers are particularly important in services where the UK is relatively strong. In the pessimistic scenario, the overall loss swells to 3.09%, with most of the impact coming from non-tariff barriers (2.55%). These far outweigh the fiscal saving.

In cash terms, the loss is £50 billion in the pessimistic scenario and still a substantial £18 billion in the optimistic scenario.

Table 1: Welfare changes in the UK if the UK leaves the EU (static model)

	Pessimistic	Optimistic
1. Increase in tradable tariffs	-0.14%	0%
2. Increase in non-tariff barriers	-0.93%	-0.40%
3. Future falls in non-tariff barriers	-2.55%	-1.26%
4. Fiscal benefit	0.53%	0.53%
5. Total welfare change	-3.09%	-1.13%

Notes: Welfare measured by change in real consumption in the UK.
Source: Ottaviano, Pessoa, Sampson and Van Reenen (2014).

Dynamic effects

These calculations highlight the losses that Brexit would cause in terms of forgone specialisation according to comparative advantage. As such, they should be interpreted as lower bounds on the total costs of Brexit. First, there are other sources of static losses from Brexit that the model does not take into account in terms of a lower variety of imported goods and services; reduced economies of scale; weakened competition and generally less exit of low productivity firms (Corcos et al, 2012).

Even more importantly, these estimates do not take into account the effects of trade on growth. Trade could increase productivity via more competition, innovation and adoption of technologies. The fact that empirical studies of big trade liberalisations usually find much larger effects of trade on output is consistent with these other mechanisms. Indeed, analysis of the EU's single market programme of the early 1990s found considerable benefits, much more than the static calculations given above would suggest.

In terms of formal quantitative dynamic models, Sampson (2014) finds that accounting for the dynamic effects of trade on technology adoption triples the static effects and Bloom et al (2014) find a doubling.

An alternative way to evaluate the impact of Brexit is to use the results of simple, less theory based empirical studies of the effects of EU membership. Baier et al (2008) find that after controlling for other determinants of bilateral trade, EU members trade substantially more with other EU countries than they do with members of EFTA. Their estimates imply that, if the UK leaves the EU and joins EFTA, its trade with countries in the EU will fall by about a quarter. Combining this with the estimates that a 1% decline in trade reduces income by between 0.5% and 0.75% (Feyrer, 2009) implies that leaving the EU (and joining EFTA) will reduce UK income by between 6.3% and 9.5%.

These estimates are much higher than the costs obtained from the static trade model, implying that the dynamic gains from trade are important. To put these numbers in perspective, during the 2008/09 global financial crisis, the UK's GDP fell by around 7% (NIESR, 2013).

The bottom line is that including these other trade effects should at least double the losses from the static case in Table 1. Hence, even under the most optimistic assumptions, we would expect a loss of 2.2% of GDP and, under pessimistic assumptions, this rises to almost 10%.

Other economic effects: regulation, immigration, foreign direct investment

The UK received the most foreign direct investment (FDI) of any European country in 2011, and was second only to the

United States in terms of the stock of inward FDI around the world (House of Commons, 2013). Part of the attraction of the UK is as an export platform to the rest of the EU, so if the UK is outside the trading bloc, this position is likely to be threatened (HM Treasury, 2010; Barrell and Pain, 1998). This matters because foreign multinationals tend to be high productivity firms and they bring new technologies and management skills with them (Bloom et al, 2012). There is also some evidence of positive spillovers from FDI in the UK (Haskel et al, 2002).

Outside the EU, the UK could restrict immigration from the rest of the EU and vice versa. Economically, migratory flows act much like trade as people tend to move to where they can be more productive and earn higher incomes, increasing total welfare. Restricting this mobility will, just like restricting trade, reduce UK overall welfare: di Giovanni et al (2012) find that the maximum size of such effects would be a loss of 1.5% of income. Other evidence suggests that there were no negative effects on jobs and wages of native Britons from the waves of EU immigration (see Wadsworth, 2014). So even on distributional grounds, immigration does not seem to have been damaging.

Currently the UK is able to influence the rules and regulations governing the EU single market. Even if the UK maintained full access to the single market, it would be in the same situation as Switzerland: UK exports would have to obey these regulations, even though the country was not party to agreeing them.

Conclusions

The costs and benefits of the UK leaving the EU are complex. Losses due to trade alone could be very substantial. Even under very optimistic assumptions, the sum of the static and dynamic trade losses would be almost 2.2% of GDP. More pessimistic calculations would lead to a long-term loss of almost a tenth of national income. The dream of splendid isolation may turn out to be a very costly one indeed.

Additional readings:

- Baier, SL, JH Bergstrand, P Egger, and PA McLaughlin (2008): 'Do Economic Integration Agreements Actually Work? Issues in Understanding the Causes and Consequences of the
- Growth of Regionalism', The World Economy 31(4): 461-97.
- Barrell, R and N Pain (1998): 'Real Exchange Rates, Agglomerations, and Irreversibilities: Macroeconomic Policy and FDI in EMU', Oxford Review of Economic Policy 14(3): 152-67.
- Bloom, N, P Romer, S Terry and J Van Reenen (2014) 'A Trapped Factors Model of Innovation', CEP Discussion Paper No. 1261
- Bloom, N, R Sadun and J Van Reenen (2012) 'Americans Do I.T Better: US Multinationals and the Productivity Miracle', American Economic Review 102(1): 167-201.
- Corcos, G, M Del Gatto, G Mion and G Ottaviano (2012) 'Productivity and Firm Selection: Quantifying the 'New' Gains from Trade', Economic Journal 122(561): 754-98.
- di Giovanni, J, A Levchenko and F Ortega (2012) 'A Global View of Cross-Border Migration', CReAM Discussion Paper No. 1218.

- Feyrer, J (2009) 'Trade and Income - Exploiting Time Series in Geography', National Bureau of Economic Research (NBER) Working Paper No. 14910.
- Haskel, J, S Pereira and M Slaughter (2002) 'Does Inward Foreign Direct Investment Boost the Productivity of Domestic Firms?', National Bureau of Economic Research (NBER). Working Paper No. 8724.
- HM Treasury (2010) 'EU Membership and FDI'
- HM Treasury (2013) 'European Union Finances 2013: Statement on the 2013 EU Budget and Measures to Counter Fraud and Financial Mismanagement'
- House of Commons (2013) 'Leaving the EU', Research Paper 13/42, 1 July 2013.
- NIESR (2013) 'Estimates of Monthly GDP'
- Ottaviano, G, J Pessoa, T Sampson and J Van Reenen (2014) 'The Costs and Benefits of Leaving the EU', CEP mimeo.
- Sampson, T (2014) 'Dynamic Selection: An Idea Flows Theory of Entry, Trade and Growth', LSE mimeo.
- Wadsworth, J (2014) 'Immigration, the European Union and the UK Labour Market' CEP Policy Analysis.

Open Europe: the economic impact of Brexit

In this study, Open Europe primarily examines the economic impact of Britain leaving the EU.

Open Europe's study draws on detailed economic modelling, showing that the economic impact of Brexit is not as clear cut in either direction as most previous analyses have suggested. Instead it will depend on a number of tough decisions in the UK and Europe. This includes whether the EU itself will embrace reform and British politicians and voters are willing to accept ambitious deregulation and new levels of competition through expansion of free trade.

-2.2%   +1.6%

Worst case scenario: Impact of Brexit on UK GDP

In a worst case scenario, where the UK fails to strike a trade deal with the rest of the EU and does not pursue a free trade agenda, Open Europe estimates that UK GDP would be 2.2% lower in 2030 than if the UK had remained inside the EU.

Source: Open Europe

Best case scenario: Impact of Brexit on UK GDP

In a best case scenario, where the UK strikes a FTA with the EU, pursues very ambitious deregulation of its economy and opens up almost fully to trade with the rest of the world, Open Europe estimates that UK GDP would be 1.6% higher in 2030 than if it had stayed within the EU.

Source: Open Europe

The numbers

Based on economic modelling of the trade impacts of Brexit and analysis of the most significant pieces of EU regulation, if Britain left the EU on 1 January 2018, we estimate that in 2030:

In a worst case scenario, where the UK fails to strike a trade deal with the rest of the EU and does not pursue a free trade agenda, Gross Domestic Product (GDP) would be 2.2% lower than if the UK had remained inside the EU.

In a best case scenario, where the UK strikes a Free Trade Agreement (FTA) with the EU, pursues very ambitious deregulation of its economy and opens up almost fully to trade with the rest of the world, UK GDP would be 1.6% higher than if it had stayed within the EU.

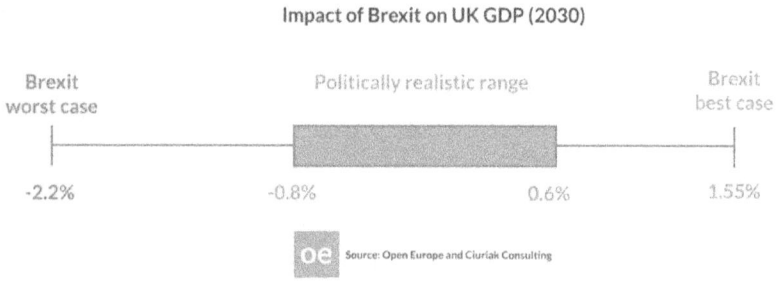

However, these are outliers. The more realistic range is between a 0.8% permanent loss to GDP in 2030 – where the UK strikes a comprehensive trade deal with the EU but does nothing else; and a 0.6% permanent gain in GDP in 2030 – where it pursues free trade with the rest of the world and deregulation, in addition to an EU FTA.

% GDP	Brexit worst case	UK-EU FTA 1	UK-EU FTA 2	Brexit best case
Initial cost	-2.76	-1.03	-1.03	-1.03
EU budget saving	0.53	0.22	0.22	0.53
Unilateral free trade	-	-	0.75	0.75
Deregulation	-	-	0.7	1.3
Total welfare gain/loss	-2.23	-0.81	0.64	1.55

Impact of various Brexit scenarios on UK GDP (2030)

Source: Open Europe and Ciuriak Consulting

The tough choices facing Britain outside

In none of our scenarios would the cost of leaving the single market and the EU customs union be off-set by merely striking a new trade deal with the EU. Britain will only prosper outside the EU if it is prepared to use its new found freedom to undertake active steps towards trade liberalisation and deregulation. It faces a series of difficult choices:

Beyond the border: Opening up the UK economy to trade with the rest of the world – including the USA, India, China and Indonesia – is essential to economic growth post-Brexit. However, this would mean exposing UK firms and workers to whole new levels of competition from low-cost countries, and would therefore be politically very sensitive.

On the border: In order to be competitive outside the EU, Britain would need to keep a liberal policy for labour migration. However, of those voters who want to leave the EU, a majority rank limiting free movement and immigration as their main motivation, meaning the UK may move in the opposite direction.

Behind the border: EU rules have largely been incorporated into UK law, and would remain in force until the UK Parliament decided to amend or scrap them. Outside the EU, we estimate that a very liberally inclined UK government could in theory cut the cost of the most burdensome EU regulations by an amount equivalent to between 0.7% and 1.3% of GDP. However, on current evidence, Britain is likely to keep many of these EU rules, for example on climate change where it has gone further than the EU standard.

The choices for Europe

The economic advantages and disadvantages of Brexit will depend to a large extent on the future relative economic dynamism of the EU. If it manages to overcome its current economic problems, and liberalises internal and external trade, then the cost of Brexit relative to remaining within the EU will be higher.

The process of leaving

Article 50 – the only established legal way to leave the EU – is a major liability. Once triggered, there is no turning back, it excludes the UK from key decisions as well as the final vote and it leaves the EU in charge of the timetable during two years of negotiations, following which the UK could be presented with a 'take it or leave it' deal. Our results show that leaving without a preferential trading agreement would dent UK GDP significantly.

Sector analysis

After initial disruption, there is a high likelihood that the UK and the EU could conclude preferential trade deals covering goods sectors, but with new border and administrative costs due to rules governing foreign content in their products. For many sectors, a deal may involve adhering to the EU's high regulatory standards.

For the remaining services sectors, and financial services in particular, guaranteeing seamless access to EU markets for UK businesses will be more difficult, not least because the UK has a deficit with the EU in goods, but a surplus in services.

Say over the rules

Though some standards are set globally, most sectors would suffer from the UK's loss of voting rights in the EU – the financial services sector in particular.

Alternative models

Open Europe judges alternatives to full EU membership on four tests – EU market access, say over the rules, gains in independence and negotiability – concluding that none of the existing models are suitable for the UK.

Source: Open Europe

Instead, the UK would likely have to negotiate a tailored deal for itself. Based on our tests, a "Single Market-Lite" arrangement – staying inside a very tightly defined EU single market – would be the most beneficial for the UK. Unlike the EEA, this must also involve voting rights over the rules governing the single market, which would be very difficult to negotiate.

A politically more realistic alternative is a comprehensive Free Trade Agreement, differing from the "Swiss model" by including better access for financial services and a fair say over how rules and standards are implemented.

The UK could also pursue unilateral liberalisation, which would involve minimum negotiations with the EU but difficult domestic political decisions. However, our modelling suggests that a strategy of agreeing FTAs with the EU and other states, followed by unilateral free trade with the rest of the world would produce the greatest benefit.

Given the difficulty in leaving the EU and the extent of the political and economic challenges the UK would need to overcome to make Brexit work in its long-term interests, it would be foolhardy to leave without first testing the limits of EU reform. Limiting the areas of EU interference and further market liberalisation would be the most beneficial option for both the UK and the EU.

How would Brexit impact the City of London?

Last February the Financial Times published an article where it exposed the potential impact of Brexit on the financial services.

According to the Financial Times[5], five are the sectors which may suffer the most from an exit from the EU, particularly over matters concerning the regulatory and tax regimes whilst the UK negotiate a new deal with the Union.

Asset management

The UK-based fund management industry accounts for a third of all the assets managed in Europe. A key to the growth of this industry has been UK companies' ability to "passport" (i.e. sell) their funds into Europe as members of the EU. Brexit would raise questions about the ability of UK-based groups to sell retail funds elsewhere in Europe.

Hedge funds

UK hedge funds would also be unable to passport their funds into the EU. However, the impact would not be too big because London-based hedge funds largely raise money from investors outside the bloc. A key area that would not change for hedge fund managers relates to restrictions on short selling and certain aspects of credit default swaps that have been subject to regulation since the financial crisis. This is because the rules relate to where the stock or instruments are listed, rather than where the fund manager is based.

---

[5] The Financial Times, "City fears loss of access and influence in event of Brexit", 5 February 2015.

Insurance

Europe's insurance market is very domestic and there is not a developed single market. It is thought Brexit would have little direct or immediate impact on the UK's insurance industry, which has a £2.8bn trade deficit with the EU.

Private equity

As with hedge funds, European investors are not a large contributor of funding to UK private equity managers. The biggest impact of Brexit on private equity would be in the area of venture capital.

Trading and settlement

London is one of the world's hubs for the vast $700tn market for over-the-counter derivatives, financial instruments that were blamed for exacerbating the financial crisis.

International rules will ensure more of this bank-dominated market is managed through clearing houses, with the aim of reducing risk.

If Britain left the EU, the European Central Bank could increase pressure for more direct oversight of all euro-denominated swaps that are currently cleared through UK-based clearing houses.

Top 100 EU rules cost Britain £33.3bn

Extract from Open Europe's analysis on the burden of EU regulation on the UK economy, and whether swapping full EU membership for EEA membership, i.e. the 'Norway Option', would be a better way to cut regulatory costs.

Based on an analysis of UK Government Impact Assessments (IAs), Open Europe estimates that the cost of the 100 most burdensome EU-derived regulations to the UK economy stands at £33.3bn a year in 2014 prices. This is more than the £27bn the UK Treasury expects to raise in revenue from Council Tax in the current (2014-15) financial year.

The top five costliest EU-derived regulations in force in the UK:

- The UK Renewable Energy Strategy – Recurring cost: £4.7bn a year
- The CRD IV package – Recurring cost: £4.6bn a year
- The Working Time Directive – Recurring cost: £4.2bn a year
- The EU Climate and Energy Package – Recurring cost: £3.4bn a year
- The Temporary Agency Workers Directive – Recurring cost: £2.1bn a year

According to the IAs, these regulations also provide a total benefit of £58.6bn a year. However, £46bn of this benefit stems from just three items, which are vastly over-stated. For example, the stated benefit of the EU's climate targets

(£20.8bn) was dependent on a global deal to reduce carbon emissions that was never struck. In fact, Open Europe estimates that up to 95% of the benefits envisaged in the impact assessment have failed to materialise.

Taking the regulations individually, the impact assessments show that Ministers signed off at least 26 of the top 100 EU-derived regulations, despite the IAs explicitly stating that the costs outweigh the estimated benefits. These regulations include the UK Temporary Agency Workers Directive and the Energy Performance of Buildings Directive.

A further 31 of the costliest EU-derived regulations have not been quantified. Between the over-stated benefits, the regulations that come with a net cost and the ones with unquantified benefits, it remains unclear how many of these EU-derived rules actually come with a net benefit in reality, showing that there is plenty of scope to cut regulatory cost to business and the public sector.

Although the cost of EU regulation too high in proportion to the benefits it generates, it is important to note that these rules can bring benefits including by facilitating trade across the single market, for example in the case of financial services rules such as MiFID.

The 'Norway option' offers minimal scope for deregulation

If the UK were to leave the EU, the costs described above would not disappear overnight – much would depend on what path Britain took outside the EU. If the UK were to leave the EU and instead 'become like Norway' by joining the European Economic Area (EEA), 93 out of these 100 costliest EU-derived regulations would remain in place at a cost of £31.4bn (94.3% of the total cost). This is because under EEA, many EU policy areas would continue to apply to the UK including financial services, social and employments laws, energy and climate change policies, and this is where the bulk of the regulatory cost stems from.

Given that EEA membership comes without any formal voting powers in the EU institutions, the UK would lose its ability to both amend these regulations and shape new EU laws.

While the 'Norway option' does mean greater independence in certain areas – chiefly the repatriation of agricultural policy, regional policy, trade policy and justice and home affairs – overall, it would make little sense to leave one club only to join another with many of the same costly rules.

EU has finally made some progress on cutting red tape

Over the last two years, the EU has taken some welcome steps to relieve the pressure of EU regulation on businesses and adopted several of Open Europe's ideas in this area. In particular, the appointment of Frans Timmermans as Vice-President of the European Commission with a responsibility for Better Regulation. Since his appointment, Timmermans has already proposed scrapping 80 out of 450 pending legislative proposals, however, there is still a long way to go, particularly in terms of addressing the existing stock of EU legislation.

Bibliography

This book is entirely based on secondary data which was collected by third parties; reviewed, analysed and reworked by the author. Sources include:

Bank of England

Open Europe

Pro Europa

The Telegraph

The Financial Times

Lisbon Treaty

EFTA

House of Commons Library

Centre for Economic Performance (CEP)

European Commission

GOV.UK Statistics

Acknowledgements

The author would like to thank everyone who has directly or indirectly contributed to the making of this book.

Special thanks go to:

James Maynard
John Wood
London School of Journalism
Mary H. Woods
Nicola Spanu

ABC Economics – Abbiamo Bisogno di Crescita

Website: http://abceconomics.com/

Email: abc.economics@yahoo.com

Facebook: https://www.facebook.com/abceconomics

Twitter: https://twitter.com/ABCEconomics

Copyright © 2015 Stefano Fugazzi

http://abceconomics.com/

www.ingramcontent.com/pod-product-compliance
Lightning Source LLC
Chambersburg PA
CBHW072229170526
45158CB00002BA/815